INFORMATION
EXPLORER
JUNIOR

Review It! Helping Peers Create Their Best Work

by Kristin Fontichiaro

CHERRY LAKE PUBLISHING · ANN ARBOR, MICHIGAN

A NOTE TO PARENTS AND TEACHERS: Please remind your children how to stay safe online before they do the activities in this book.

A NOTE TO KIDS: Always remember your safety comes first!

Published in the United States of America
by Cherry Lake Publishing
Ann Arbor, Michigan
www.cherrylakepublishing.com

Content Adviser: Gail Dickinson, PhD, Professor,
Old Dominion University, Norfolk, Virginia

Photo Credits: Cover, © wavebreakmedia/Shutterstock.com; page 5, © D. Maria/
Shutterstock.com; page 9, © MaIII Themd/Shutterstock.com; page 10, ©
Pressmaster/Shutterstock.com; pages 14 and 15, © racorn/Shutterstock.com.

Library of Congress Cataloging-in-Publication Data
Fontichiaro, Kristin.
  Review it! : helping peers create their best work / by Kristin Fontichiaro.
    pages cm. — (Information explorer junior)
  Includes bibliographical references and index.
  ISBN 978-1-63188-865-6 (lib. bdg.) — ISBN 978-1-63188-877-9 (pbk.) —
ISBN 978-1-63188-889-2 (pdf) —ISBN 978-1-63188-901-1 (e-book)
  1. Editing—Juvenile literature. 2. Peer teaching—Juvenile literature. 3. Report
writing—Evaluation—Juvenile literature. 4. English language—Composition and
exercises—Evaluation—Juvenile literature. 5. School prose—Evaluation—Juvenile
literature. I. Title.

  PN162.F66 2015
  372.62'3—dc23   2014024987

Cherry Lake Publishing would like to acknowledge the work of The Partnership
for 21st Century Skills. Please visit www.p21.org for more information.

Printed in the United States of America
Corporate Graphics Inc.
January 2015

Table of Contents

CHAPTER ONE

What Is Peer Editing?

During your life, you will do a lot of writing. You might write stories or reports for school. You could write letters asking people for help or for a job. Maybe you will write directions to help kids put together toys or teach people how to play board games. You might even write commercials or scripts for TV or the Internet.

We write to share what we are thinking. When we write, our ideas and words should make sense to the people reading them.

Have you ever written a birthday or other card to a friend?

Good peer editing is positive and helpful.

Learning to be a better writer takes a lot of practice. That is why we spend so much time writing in school. Sometimes, your teacher will give you advice on how to make your writing better. But sometimes, it is helpful to get feedback from other kids. When you read someone else's paper and give advice about it, you are doing **peer editing**. A peer is someone who is like you. This might be a classmate or another person your age.

Someone who lives in the same place or does the same activities as you can also be a peer.

Whenever we are given someone else's writing, we are being asked to tell that person what we think of their creation. We want to help them do their best. But we do not want to hurt their feelings. That means we need to act with **empathy**. We want to help but not punish. Tell the truth, but nicely. Good peer editing means you balance suggestions for what to change with **praise** or compliments. One easy way to do that is to read your classmate's paper three times. Each time, you focus on something different. You'll learn more about this method in the next pages.

Use praise to keep your suggestions from being too negative.

Suggestions

Praise

To get a copy of this activity, visit www.cherrylakepublishing.com/activities.

Try This

Writing is everywhere! Talk to at least three adults. Ask them how they use writing in their jobs. Do they ever look at the writing of their coworkers or other peers? Make a list of all the kinds of writing and reviewing they do. Combine your list with those of other kids in your class. How long a list can your class make?

CHAPTER TWO

Helpful Praise

When someone asks you to read their writing, ask them what the **purpose** of their writing is. Is it to:

- Share facts?
- Follow a writing pattern?
- **Persuade**?
- Describe an event or object?
- Use exciting, "juicy" words?
- Practice capital letters?

The answers to these questions will help you know what kind of feedback to give.

Now think about the last time your teacher gave you back a piece of writing. There were probably some corrections on it and a few compliments. Which did you want to see first? Probably the compliments!

Mia asks her friend Tom to peer edit a paper she wrote for school. The first time Tom reads Mia's paper, he helps her find the parts that are really great. He looks for interesting and wonderful ideas, words, and writing. Maybe Mia describes sunlight in a beautiful way. Perhaps she uses a juicy word such as "dappled" instead of a simple word such as "sunny." Tom makes those great ideas stand out!

Choosing just the right words can help readers create a strong image in their minds. What juicy words could you use to describe the sunlight? The mist? The green crops?

For this part, you can use a highlighter or colored pencil. If you peer edit on the computer, you can find the highlighting feature on your computer program. Underline or highlight those great ideas so they stand out. Tom grabs his favorite highlighter. He takes his first look at Mia's personal narrative about what she does when it is raining.

A brightly colored marker is a great way to mark the best parts of something you are reading.

When it is a rainy day, I like to ==relax== at my house. I like to ==stretch out like a Lion== on my couch. I get a good book and start reading Sometimes, my brother and I play a game together. Before we know it, the sun is out. we can go back outside. ==Hello, sun!==

Tom highlights "relax." He thinks it is a more interesting word than "rest," which also would have worked there. He highlights "stretch out like a Lion," too. It helped him get a picture in his mind about what Mia looked like. He also highlights, "Hello, sun!" It was a cheerful way to end the narrative.

When Mia gets her writing back, she will feel great. Those orange marks mean, "You did great here!"

To get a copy of this activity, visit www.cherrylakepublishing.com/activities.

Try This

Fred was asked to write a how-to paragraph about skiing. Make a copy of the paragraph below and highlight the best parts.

Winter is wonderful. The snow is bright, and the sun is smiling. Time to ski! First, point your ski tips together. Your skis should look like a pizza! Next, push into the snow with your poles. Third, point your feet downhill. Gently turn from side to side. Feel the wind brushing your face. If you feel like you are going too fast, push your skis together and lean in. That will help you stop. Finally, you reach the bottom of the hill. You did it!

STOP!
Don't write in the book!

CHAPTER THREE

Suggesing Improvements

Tom is done with the first round of edits. Now, he looks for places where the writing could be better. He also looks for places where he might want to leave an **encouraging** message for Mia. When you peer edit, remember to think about the writer's purpose. What did the writer intend to do? How can you help the writer do this better?

Always be sure that your criticism is friendly and helpful.

Tom makes a quick list of what he needs to look for on his second read:

- Words or ideas that could be added
- Words or phrases that could be replaced by more interesting or descriptive words
- Ideas or descriptions that need to be clearer or that confuse him as the reader

On this review, Tom is looking for problems. But he still wants to point them out in a helpful way. When peer editing, you want to use helpful language. Remember that it is hard to hear criticism. Don't be mean!

For the second read, you need a pen that is a different color from the writing. Tom decides to use a red pen, but any color is okay! Just make it a color that stands out from the writing. This is so the author can see it easily. Write notes to the author in the margins, the white space on the edges of the

Your notes should offer ideas for ways your peer can improve her work.

paper. If you are reading on the computer, ask your teacher or librarian how to use the New Comment feature to make comments. Write enough words so that your ideas make sense to the author.

As Tom reads Mia's paper the second time, he carefully adds comments in red.

When it is a rainy day, I like to relax at my house. I like to stretch out like a Lion on my coach. I get a good book and start reading Sometimes, my brother and I play a game together. Before we know it, the sun is out. we can go back outside. Hello, sun!

Great! This helps me imagine what you look and feel like.

What do you read? Maybe tell us what kinds of books you like on a rainy day.

Do you get along during the game? Or do you fight?

I like this. It sounds like you are excited to see the sun again!

To get a copy of this activity, visit www.cherrylakepublishing.com/activities.

Try This

Rory wrote the description below of her dog. Copy the paragraph on another piece of paper. Go through and highlight the parts you like most. Then add some margin comments so Rory knows how to make it better.

My dog's name is Greta. She is a beagle. Her fur feels silky. She likes being petted. She does not bark very much. She begs for treats. Ice cream is her favorite food. She puts her paws up on the chair. When she sleeps, she snores like a train. I love her very much.

ICE CREAM

STOP! Don't write in the book!

CHAPTER FOUR

Punctuation, Capital Letters, and Spelling

So far, Tom has pointed out what is great about the ideas and where Mia could improve. Now it is time for Tom to think like a **copyeditor**. A copyeditor is someone who looks closely at spelling and at punctuation. Professional authors who write the books and magazines you read rely on copyeditors to find mistakes before their words are printed on paper or on-screen. Copyeditors use special codes or symbols. Using codes saves time and helps the copyeditor communicate quickly with authors. For example, it is much faster to use the bullet symbol than to write, "Please add a period here."

When doing this part, you might want to use a new pen color, too. That will make your changes easy to see.

Here are three symbols that you might use when copyediting someone's writing on paper:

/   Use a lower case letter instead.

≡   capitalize this letter

⊙   add a period

If you are copyediting on the computer, ask your teacher or librarian to show you how to turn on the Track Changes feature. With this feature turned on, you can change the punctuation, spelling, or capital letters yourself. The computer puts your changes in a different color so they stand out to your author.

If a word is spelled wrong, cross it out. Then write in the correct spelling above it. If you think a word is spelled wrong but do not know how to spell it, circle the word. Write "sp" next to it. This is a shortcut for, "Spelling mistake?"

When Tom adds copyediting codes to Mia's paper, it looks like this:

When it is a rainy day, I like to relax at my house. I like to stretch out like a lion on my

couch
~~coach~~. I get a good book and start reading. Sometimes, my brother and I play a game together. Before we know it, the sun is out. we can go back outside. Hello, sun!

Great! This helps me imagine what you look and feel like.

What do you read? Maybe tell us what kinds of books you like on a rainy day.

Do you get along during the game? Or do you fight?

I like this. It sounds like you are excited to see the sun again!

Now you know how to be a good peer editor and how to help your friends and classmates write better. Good luck!

Try This

To get a copy of this activity, visit www.cherrylakepublishing.com/activities.

Before you practice on a friend's paper, help Diego with his paragraph! What edits would you suggest? Remember to read it three times:

1. Highlight or underline the best parts.
2. Make suggestions or compliments in the margins.
3. Switch pens and correct spelling, punctuation, and writing mistakes.

Are you ready for a pet? my mom says that you have to take care of your pet every day She says your pett is like your babby. You have to feed it and make sure it is happy. you Have to keep it healthy, too. If that sounds like too much work, then do not get a Pet!

STOP!
Don't write in the book!

21

Glossary

copyeditor (KAH-pee-ed-i-tur) a person who reads writing and corrects mistakes in spelling and punctuation

empathy (EM-puh-thee) thinking about how the other person is feeling or will feel

encouraging (in-KUR-i-jing) positive and supportive

peer editing (PEER ED-i-ting) reading and giving feedback on the writing of people like you, such as when a student corrects the writing of another student

persuade (pur-SWADE) make someone do or believe something by giving the person good reasons

praise (PRAYZ) words of approval or admiration

purpose (PUR-pus) a goal or aim

Find Out More

BOOKS

Minden, Cecilia, and Kate Roth. *How to Write a How-To.* Ann Arbor, MI: Cherry Lake Publishing, 2012.

Truesdell, Ann. *Find New Words with Dictionaries.* Ann Arbor, MI: Cherry Lake Publishing, 2012.

Yomtov, Nel. *How to Write a Memoir.* Ann Arbor, MI: Cherry Lake Publishing, 2014.

WEB SITES

ReadWriteThink—Editing Checklist for Self- and Peer Editing

www.readwritethink.org/classroom-resources/printouts/editing -checklist-self-peer-30232.html

Not sure what to think about when you are editing someone's writing? Use this worksheet.

Tappan Middle School—Revising and Editing

www.aaps.k12.mi.us/tappan.rothl/revising_and_editing

Want to learn more symbols you can use when you are copyediting? Check out this list from a teacher in the Ann Arbor Public Schools.

Index

About the Author

Kristin Fontichiaro teaches at the University of Michigan. She peer edits almost every day.